Uncharted, Unexplored, and Unexplained

Scientific Advancements of the 19th Century

SAYVILLE LIBRARY

Pierre and Marie Curie

and the Discovery of Radium

Mitchell Lane
PUBLISHERS

P.O. Box 196
Hockessin,
Delaware 19707

Uncharted, Unexplored, and Unexplained

Scientific Advancements of the 19th Century

Titles in the Series

Visit us on the web: www.mitchelllane.com
Comments? email us: mitchelllane@mitchelllane.com

Uncharted, Unexplored, and Unexplained

Scientific Advancements of the 19th Century

Pierre and Marie Curie

and the Discovery of Radium

by Kathleen Tracy

Uncharted, Unexplored, and Unexplained

Scientific Advancements of the 19th Century

Mitchell Lane
PUBLISHERS

Printing   1   2   3   4   5   6   7   8
    Library of Congress Cataloging-in-Publication Data
Tracy, Kathleen.
    Pierre and Marie Curie and the discovery of radium / Kathleen Tracy.
        p. cm. — (Uncharted, unexplored & unexplained)
    Includes bibliographical references and index.
    ISBN 1-58415-310-5 (lib. bdg.)
        1. Curie, Pierre, 1859–1906—Juvenile literature. 2. Curie, Marie, 1867–1934—Juvenile literature. 3. Chemists—France—Biography—Juvenile literature. 4. Chemists—Poland—Biography—Juvenile literature. 5. Radioactivity—History—Juvenile literature. I. Title. II. Series.
QD22.C82T73 2005
540'.92'244—dc22

                                                                            2004002051

ABOUT THE AUTHOR: Kathleen Tracy has been a journalist for over twenty years. Her writing has been featured in magazines including *The Toronto Star*'s "Star Week," *A Biography* magazine, *KidScreen* and *TV Times*. She is also the author of numerous biographies including, "The Boy Who Would be King" (Dutton), "Jerry Seinfeld—The Entire Domain" (Carol Publishing), "Don Imus—America's Cowboy" (Carroll), "Mariano Guadalupe Vallejo," and "William Hewlett: Pioneer of the Computer Age," both for Mitchell Lane. She recently completed *Diana Rigg: The Biography* for Benbella Books.
PHOTO CREDITS: Cover, pp. 1, 3, 26—American Institute of Physics; p. 6—T. A. Mousseau/University of South Carolina; p. 8—The General Libraries/University of Texas at Austin; pp. 12, 14, 16, 22, 28, 41—Archives Curie et Joloit-Curie, Paris; pp. 18, 19—Marie Sklodowska Curie Museum; p. 30—*Die Berühmten Erfinder, Physiker, und Ingenieure*, Aulis Verlag Deubner, Köln, Germany; pp. 31, 33—Liverpool Middle School; p. 33—The Red Green and Blue Company/The Element Collection; pp. 32, 36, 38—Yale University School of Medicine; p. 34—The Burns Archive; p. 39—Corbis; p. 39—Rochester Institute of Technology/Center for Imaging Science; p. 40—The Paris Pages/www.paris.org.
PUBLISHER'S NOTE: This story is based on the author's extensive research, which she believes to be accurate. Documentation of such research is contained on page 47.

Uncharted, Unexplored, and Unexplained

Scientific Advancements of the 19th Century

Pierre and Marie Curie

and the Discovery of Radium

*For Your Information

The world's worst nuclear accident occurred in 1986 at Chernobyl in the Soviet Union. Thousands of people eventually died from radiation poisoning. The accident contaminated the area around Chernobyl and forced more than 90,000 people from their homes. Today, the area is still highly radioactive.

1

A Deadly Accident

It was early in the morning of Saturday, April 26, 1986. Workers at the Chernobyl nuclear power plant in the Soviet Union were getting ready for work. Most had started their shifts at midnight. They rode to work in buses that picked them up in the nearby town of Pripyat. The Chernobyl plant had four reactors that were capable of producing enough electricity to provide power to over seven million people. There were plans to build two more reactors on the site. Chernobyl was considered the pride of the Russian nuclear energy program. Local residents welcomed the plant because it provided people in the nearby towns with steady employment.

Although it was after midnight, the air was comfortably warm. A team of workers prepared to conduct an experiment on reactor No. 4. They wanted to find out whether it was possible, in the event of a power outage, to use the reactor's own power to supply electricity to water pumps that cooled the reactors' uranium fuel rods. The test had to be run when the reactor's power was low, so they scheduled the experiment for when No. 4 was going through a routine shutdown for regular maintenance.

Prior to the experiment, the operators decreased the power to reactor No. 4's turbines. To their surprise, the reactor grew unstable. First, there was an unexpected increase in steam. That led to a power surge, which in turn led to more steam. Viktor Haynes and Marko Bojcun, authors of *The Chernobyl Disaster*, describe what happened next: "The 1,661 fuel rods, now

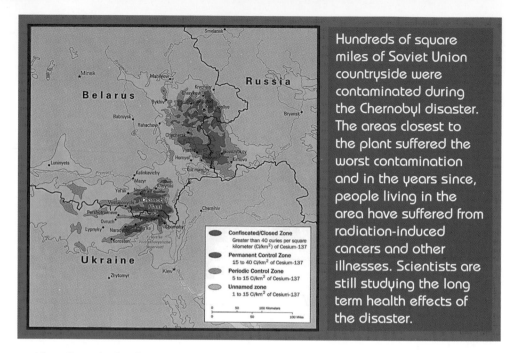

Hundreds of square miles of Soviet Union countryside were contaminated during the Chernobyl disaster. The areas closest to the plant suffered the worst contamination and in the years since, people living in the area have suffered from radiation-induced cancers and other illnesses. Scientists are still studying the long term health effects of the disaster.

red-hot from lack of coolant, disintegrated in powder and fragments and under immense pressure, broke through their cladding into outer steam-water enclosures."[1]

The walls and floors began to shake. Then a massive explosion rocked reactor No. 4. The blast was so powerful that the 225-foot-high concrete wall surrounding the reactor was destroyed. The reactor's one-thousand-ton, or two-million-pound, steel lid collapsed in pieces. Radioactive sediment was hurled through the walls and roof. Huge chunks of uranium were propelled into the ground and sky. Oil and electrical fires broke out everywhere. Moments later, oxygen-rich night air rushed in through the destroyed walls. When the air combined with the reactor's radioactive material, a second explosion boomed through the night. A massive fireball soared toward the heavens. The resulting mushroom cloud spread over the area. Everyone knew a catastrophe of almost unimaginable proportions had just occurred. The amount of radiation released into the environment was more than two hundred times greater than the amount released in the World War II bombings of Hiroshima and Nagasaki combined. And as the radioactive particles made their way skyward, winds blew them across Russia and on into Europe.

The fire that raged in the reactor's core burned at temperatures of up to 5000 degrees Fahrenheit, twice that of molten steel. Between the heat and the radioactivity, it was impossible to get near the fire on the ground to put it out. Eventually, it was controlled by helicopters dropping special fire retardants on the reactor.

In all, an estimated 91,000 people were evacuated from their homes. They were only allowed to take what possessions they could carry. They would never return. Thirty-two people died in the initial explosions from exposure to massive amounts of radiation. People in the Ukraine, Belarus, and Russia received the worst of the nuclear fallout. They were afflicted with the largest dose of radioactivity in history. Thousands died later from effects of the accident. Many died from a variety of radiation-related cancers, such as leukemia. By 1995, there were 800 cases of thyroid cancer reported in children who had been under fifteen years old at the time of the accident. The Ukrainian government believes hundreds of thousands of people have continued to suffer from Chernobyl-related Illnesses. Among these is former Olympic gymnastics gold medallist Olga Korbut. She lived 130 miles from the plant.

A disaster like Chernobyl reminds us of the awesome power of radiation. But the fact is we live surrounded by it every day of our lives. Radiation is a form of energy that has a very short wavelength. It is part of the same wavelength spectrum that includes X-rays and infrared, ultraviolet, and visible light. Radiation brings us everyday radio waves and microwaves. But the shorter the wavelength gets, the more energy the radiation has. X-rays and radiation with wavelengths shorter than X-rays, such as gamma rays, are emitted by a number of radioactive elements. They are so powerful they can penetrate human tissue. That is why radiation can be deadly.

Earth is full of natural radioactive elements and has been since it was born. The planet is also bombarded every day with radiation from outer space, like an invisible drizzle of rain. Charged particles from the sun and stars interact with Earth's atmosphere and magnetic field to produce a steady shower of radiation. This is typically beta and gamma radiation. But the doses, or amounts, of cosmic radiation available to be absorbed by a person or an object vary depending on what part of the world it falls. Differences in elevation and the effects of Earth's magnetic field can affect cosmic radiation levels.

Radioactive material found on Earth occurs naturally in soil, water, and vegetation. The best-known source of Earth's radiation is the element uranium and some of its isotopes. An isotope is a form of an element that has a different number of neutrons than the element itself. Small amounts of uranium and its isotopes are found everywhere. There are minute amounts in our food and water. Even humans have radioactive isotopes of elements such as potassium and lead inside their bodies from the time they are born. So radiation by itself isn't necessarily dangerous. However, it is if someone is exposed to a lot in close range over a very short period of time. This is what happened to the people living in Pripyat.

Despite radiation being everywhere, it was only a little over a century ago that scientists identified radioactivity. After that they began to understand its properties and its potential, both good and bad. Wilhelm Conrad Roentgen discovered the first clue that there might be invisible rays in the atmosphere. On the evening of November 8, 1895, Roentgen was working at the University of Wurzburg. He was experimenting with electric discharges in vacuum tubes. He noticed that a piece of paper coated with a barium compound started to glow when he set it near the tube.

He was mystified as to why the paper was glowing. Roentgen covered the gas tube with a piece of cardboard, but the paper still glowed. In a flash of understanding, he suspected that he had discovered an invisible ray. The ray had the ability to penetrate the cardboard. He immediately set out to prove his theory. He spent two months conducting experiments. Roentgen learned that the thicker or denser the object, the less the rays penetrated it. But his most dramatic discovery came when he inserted his wife's hand into the rays. Her bones could be clearly seen on the paper.

Roentgen named the mystery rays X-rays. Almost immediately they became important in medicine. X-rays gave doctors a nonsurgical way to "see" inside the human body. A devout humanitarian, Roentgen refused to patent his discovery. He believed it was more important for the world to benefit from his findings than for him to make money from them.

Roentgen's work with X-rays would set the stage for the discovery of radioactivity, which would create a new branch of science and would make a pair of brilliant chemists one of the most famous scientist couples of all time.

FYInfo

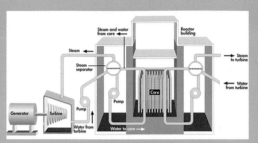

Reactor Design

Many countries, including the United States, partially depend on nuclear power. But operating nuclear reactors always carries the risk of a major accident like the one that happened at Chernobyl. Following is a list of some of the close calls the nuclear power industry has endured.

December 12, 1952. The first known major malfunction of a nuclear power plant occurred at Chalk River, Canada. It happened after the accidental removal of four control rods in an experimental nuclear power reactor. Removing the rods led to a partial meltdown of the reactor's uranium fuel core. A million gallons of radioactive water accumulated inside. Luckily, there were no injuries reported.

October 7, 1957. Workers were unable to extinguish a fire that broke out at a plutonium production plant near Liverpool, England. Two hundred square miles of countryside were contaminated. Concerned officials banned the sale of milk from cows grazing in the area for more than a month. The government would later estimate that at least 33 cancer deaths could be traced to the effects of the accident.

January 3, 1961. Near Idaho Falls, Idaho, three servicemen removed control rods from the core of an experimental military reactor by mistake. It caused a fatal steam explosion. The three servicemen were killed. These were the first fatalities in the history of U.S. nuclear reactor operations.

March 22, 1975. A worker at the Browns Ferry reactor near Decatur, Alabama, used a candle to inspect for leaks. He accidentally started a fire. The fire caused the reactor's cooling water to drop to dangerous levels. Fortunately, no radioactive material escaped into the atmosphere.

March 28, 1979. The biggest nuclear accident in the United States occurred at Three Mile Island, near Harrisburg, Pennsylvania. A combination of equipment malfunctions and human error caused one of two reactors to lose its coolant. The radioactive fuel overheated, leading to a partial meltdown. Although some radioactive material escaped, a potentially major disaster was averted. Miraculously, nobody died. The long-term effects on local residents who were exposed are still being debated.

Marie Curie had two daughters with Pierre—Eve, on the left, and Irène, who would also eventually pursue a career in science. Like many modern women, Marie was a working mom who juggled raising her children with her job as a physics instructor at the Normal Superior School for girls in Sévres, France.

2

Early Loss

Maria Sklodowska was born in Warsaw, Poland, on November 7, 1867. Warsaw was in the part of Poland that had been under Russian rule for over seventy years. The country had lost its independence in 1795 when Austria, Prussia, and czarist Russia had divided Poland's land among them. A revolt four years before Maria's birth had resulted in a harsh crackdown. As a result, an effort was made by the Russian leader to stamp out traditional Polish culture and language. The social and political climate in Poland would have a great influence on young Maria. Her parents, Bronislawa and Vladislav, were teachers. They were also Polish patriots. They did whatever they could to preserve their Polish heritage.

Maria was called Manya by her family. She was the youngest of five children. After her birth, Bronislawa quit her job as the headmistress of a girl's school. Caring for four daughters and a son and running the school was too much work. Vladislav had a good-paying job teaching math and physics at a boy's high school, so even without Bronislawa's income, the family maintained a comfortable lifestyle.

In 1871 Vladislav's brother came to stay with Manya and her family. He was not a healthy man. They didn't know it, but Manya's uncle had tuberculosis, or TB, one of the deadliest diseases of the nineteenth century. It was greatly feared because it spread so easily from person to person.

When Manya was four, Bronislawa was diagnosed with TB. Although they couldn't know for sure, they assumed she contracted it from her brother-in-law. In those days TB was incurable, and he had died from the disease. There was also no medical treatment for TB. Instead people were sent away for "cures" to warm climates. Bronislawa and her oldest daughter, Zosia, were sent away when Manya was still very young. As a result, Manya had little close contact with her mother. Even when Bronislawa was at home, she was isolated from the rest of the family in her own room.

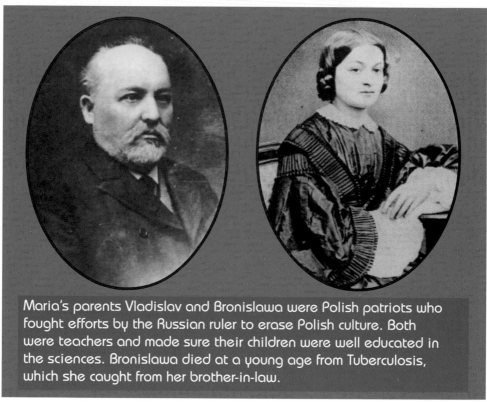

Maria's parents Vladislav and Bronislawa were Polish patriots who fought efforts by the Russian ruler to erase Polish culture. Both were teachers and made sure their children were well educated in the sciences. Bronislawa died at a young age from Tuberculosis, which she caught from her brother-in-law.

The family was very upset by Bronislawa's illness. Making things worse, Vladislav's pro-Polish stance came to the attention authorities. The Russian supervisor in charge of the school fired Vladislav. The only jobs Vladislav could find paid very little money. It became impossible to properly provide for his family. To earn extra money, the Sklodowskas took in student boarders. This led to another tragedy. Zosia caught typhus, another deadly disease, from a boarder and died. The grief over Zosia's death affected

Bronislawa's condition even more. Her health worsened. She died in 1878, at just forty-two years old. Ten-year-old Manya was devastated. Later she would call it "the first great sorrow of my life," which "threw me into a profound depression."[1] The loss of her sister and mother had a life-changing effect on the young girl. It made her both turn away from religion and turn toward a fervent belief in science and medicine. She began to dream about becoming a scientist. She wanted to find cures and help people.

Vladislav was a progressive thinker. He believed girls should be just as educated as boys. Part of his belief was political. He viewed education as a powerful weapon against the Russians. This philosophy was called Polish positivism. It emphasized science as one way of changing the world for the better. Many Polish teachers risked their jobs to participate in this movement. Their students were well aware what was at stake. "Constantly held in suspicion and spied upon, the children knew that a single conversation in Polish, or an imprudent word, might seriously harm not only themselves, but also their families,"[2] Maria would later remember.

The Russian authorities kept a close eye on the schools. Still, teachers continued teaching the Polish language and Polish history in secret. At the private grammar school that Maria attended, the students had a "double curriculum." Whenever one of the Russian inspectors was around, the children would study Russian-approved subjects. Then when he went away, the Polish textbooks would be used.

Maria was the top student of her class. She found it easy to learn both her approved subjects and the secret subjects. But her father had money problems, so he was forced to send her to a Russian-controlled public school. Maria made the transition with ease. She actually enjoyed the school. Like her brother and sisters before her, Maria would graduate number one in her class.

Maria was proud to get the gold medal for being the valedictorian of her class. But after graduating, Maria seemed emotionally exhausted. For a long time she had been depressed about her mother's death. She had also felt pressure to meet her father's academic expectations. The strain of both had finally taken their toll. Vladislav realized his daughter needed a break. He sent Maria and her older sister Helena to stay with a wealthy uncle and his family. Maria ended up staying there a year. In the summer she would go horseback riding and fishing. In the winter, she and her cousins would go on sleigh rides. She attended dances. She also got to meet many famous Polish intellectuals, who would visit her uncle's estate. There were no tests to study for, no pressure to succeed. Maria would later recall that time the only carefree year of her life.

As a young girl, Maria was an excellent student. She was always the top student in her classes and enjoyed the process of learning. After watching her mother and sister die, Maria decided she wanted to pursue a career in science so she could help find cures to diseases and help humanity. But family money troubles would delay her education.

When Maria returned to Warsaw, she was ready to resume her former lifestyle. She felt strong enough to face the challenges it posed. She had her heart set on earning an advanced degree—but it would not be easy. The University of Warsaw and all other Polish colleges did not allow women to enroll. If she stayed in Poland, the most she could hope for was to teach at a girls' school, just as her mother had. Both Maria and her sister Bronia dreamed of studying in Paris, where there was a very large Polish population. But their father had lost the family's entire savings in a bad investment. There was no money to study abroad.

Maria was not easily discouraged. She came up with a plan that would benefit both her and her sister. She and Bronia made a pact: First, Maria would get a job as a private tutor. She would help pay for Bronia to attend medical school in Paris. In return, once Bronia had her degree, she would help pay for Maria to go to college.

Although Maria's dream of attending college was on hold, it didn't mean her education stopped. Driven by an insatiable need to learn, she participated in an organization called Flying University. It was a secret academy for young women who wanted to take college-level courses but couldn't afford to go to school in another country. Classes were held in different homes around the city so that Russian authorities wouldn't discover what they were doing. According to author Naomi Pasachoff, Maria would later recall, "We agreed among ourselves to give evening courses, each one teaching what he knew best."[3] In addition, professionals would come to instruct the girls. Maria attended science classes. On the weekends she was allowed to perform physics and chemistry experiments at the Museum of Industry and Agriculture, where her cousin Jozef Boguski was the director.

Over the next two years, Maria spent her time attending classes and working as a tutor. Finding that tutoring didn't bring in much money, she took a job as a governess. She cared for the children of a wealthy businessman. He owned a beet-sugar factory in a village about ninety miles outside of Warsaw. Although she worried about living so far from her father, Maria enjoyed her job. During her time off, her employer encouraged Maria to help the children of the local peasants learn how to read. She did it even though it was forbidden by Russian authorities. If caught, Maria might have gone to prison or been sent to Siberia.

Maria liked the family she worked for, but at times she would feel frustrated. She wondered if she would ever make it to Paris.

After a while, Maria fell in love with her boss's son. His name was Kazimierz. Suddenly, Paris seemed much less important than getting married.

It was not to be. Kazimierz's parents liked Maria as a person, but because her family had no money, they thought she was unsuitable to marry their son. Maria was heartbroken. What made the situation even harder to bear was that she had to continue working for the family another year.

To help her sister pay for college, Maria worked as a governess for a wealthy man's family for a couple of years. During her time there, she continued to study on her own and discovered she had a special love for math and physics and decided to make those her primary fields of study once she started studying in Paris.

Most people would have quit rather than remain in such a painful situation, but Maria couldn't break her promise to Bronia. She needed to keep the job. "There were some very difficult days, and I will certainly count them among the cruelest in my life," she admitted years later. "The only thing that makes the memory of them easier to bear is that in spite of everything, I came out of it all honorably, with my head held high."[4]

At the time, though, every day was a struggle. To distract herself from the hurt she was feeling, Maria delved back into books and learning. She studied everything from literature to physics and chemistry. Through letters, she had her father teach her math. She took lessons from a chemist who worked at the beet-sugar factory. Maria later said, "During those years of isolated work, trying little by little to find my real preferences, I finally turned towards mathematics and physics."[5]

Maria returned to Warsaw in 1889. While she had been away, Vladislav had gotten a job. He ran a reform school. He was earning enough money that he could start paying Maria back all the money she had been sending to her sister. Meanwhile, Bronia had married a Polish doctor. She insisted Maria come live with them. She wanted Maria to continue her education in Paris. At her sister's urging, Maria finally made the move. All those years of patience and work were finally paying off.

While working as a governess in the house pictured above, Maria fell in love with the family's son, Kazimierz. She dreamed of marrying him but Kazimierz's father forbid it because Maria's family had no money. Marie was heartbroken but rather than quit, she continued working there for another year, because she had promised to help her sister Bronia pay for school.

The trip to France was long and uncomfortable. Maria bought the cheapest ticket available. The ticket did not provide an actual seat. She brought her own folding chair, a blanket, food, and enough reading material for the trip.

Maria arrived in Paris in November 1891. She enrolled at the Sorbonne. There she changed her name to Marie, the French spelling of Maria. At twenty-four years old, she was eager to make up for lost time. To enroll in the School of Sciences, Marie had to pass an entrance exam. She was one of only twenty-three young women out of almost two thousand students. She spent the next several years becoming fluent in French and earning degrees in physics and mathematics. "It was like a new world opened to me, the world of science, which I was at last permitted to know in all liberty,"[6] she wrote in her memoir.

Marie stayed at her sister's house in the beginning, but she moved out after a short time. For one reason, it was an hour's commute each way between the house and the Sorbonne. Plus, it was hard to concentrate there. Bronia's husband, Kazimierz Dulski, was a physician. During the day he worked at his medical practice. At night he ran a free clinic out of their small apartment. Dulski was also a Polish activist. His political friends were constantly stopping by. Marie's father had warned her not to get too involved with Polish ex-patriots. Ex-patriots were people who had moved away from their native country to escape the political or social climate there. Polish ex-patriots wanted to escape Russian repression. Vladislav worried Marie would become known as a radical. That could hurt her chances of securing a good job when she returned to Poland.

Marie rented a cramped attic in a well-known area near the Sorbonne called the Latin Quarter. This neighborhood attracted both artists and students. During the winter, the attic was cold and drafty. Marie had to wear several layers of clothes to stay warm. Money was tight. Her meals consisted mainly of buttered bread and hot tea. Sometimes she didn't eat at all. She would get so engrossed in her studies, she would sometimes forget to have dinner.

After earning her degrees, Marie got a job in a lab. It was run by Gabriel Lippmann, who would go on to win the Nobel Prize for physics in 1908 for developing a method to take color photographs. Eventually her work with Lippmann earned her a commission by the Society for the Encouragement of National Industry to do a study on the magnetic properties of steel. All she needed was lab space where she could work. A Polish physicist introduced Marie to a colleague he thought might be able to help. Pierre Curie was well known for his work on magnetism. He was also laboratory chief at the Municipal School of Industrial Physics and Chemistry in Paris.

Before long, he would also become the romantic love of Marie's life and her lifelong professional partner.

Czar Alexander

During Marie's childhood, Poland was under the rule of Russia. At the time, Russia was led by an emperor, or czar. Czar Alexander was born in Moscow on April 17, 1818. Although he had grown up as the privileged heir to the throne, he had to undergo difficult military training that permanently damaged his health. He assumed the throne on February 19, 1855, after his father died. Russia was in the middle of the Crimean War. The conflict pitted Russia against the Ottoman Empire, England, and France. The countries were fighting over control of land in the Middle East. A year later, Alexander signed the Treaty of Paris, which ended the war. Then he turned his energies toward improving Russia's economy.

Up until then, Russia still relied on serfs, farm laborers who worked land owned by wealthy families in exchange for food and a place to live. Alexander realized Russia needed to modernize. In 1861 he abolished serfdom. He also announced that all peasants had the right to buy land from their landlord—over the bitter objections of the noble classes.

Alexander also changed Russia's foreign policy. In 1867, he sold Alaska and the Aleutian Islands to the United States. He also concentrated on the countries in Eastern Europe under Russian control. In Poland, he initially gave Poles partial self-rule. Unhappy with the arrangement, the Poles revolted in 1863. The czar responded with brutal suppression. It was in this atmosphere of political oppression that Maria grew up.

Alexander had tried to improve the lives of the peasants, but many landowners refused to abide by the new laws. Frustrated peasants grew angry and formed secret groups. They demanded that all the land be turned over to them. Some peasant groups believed the only way to force change was through violence. As a result, Alexander was the target of several assassination attempts.

On March 1, 1881, the czar was traveling in a carriage when radicals throwing bombs attacked him. The bombs missed the carriage but exploded among some Cossacks who were guarding the czar. Alexander insisted on getting out of the carriage to check on their wounds. An assassin saw him and threw another bomb. It instantly killed the czar, as well as the assassin. Five other conspirators were later hanged. The seeds of what would become the bloody Russian revolution had been sown.

Pierre Curie is pictured here with his brother Jacques, and parents Claire and Eugene. The Curies were a tight-knit family and Pierre enjoyed a happy childhood. He developed a fascination with science at a young age and would often spend his days hiking, looking for interesting plants to take home and study with his father.

3

Magnetic Attraction

Pierre Curie was born in Paris on May 15, 1859. His mother, Claire, had grown up near Paris. Her family had once been well to do, but they lost their wealth after some social and political unrest in the late 1840s. Pierre's father, Eugène, had wanted to pursue a career in scientific research. However, he needed to earn enough money to support his family, so he gave up his dream. Instead, he set up a private medical practice.

Although the Curies lived modestly, Pierre would later tell Marie that his parents were "exquisite." He had only warm and happy memories of growing up. Like his father, Pierre loved nature and science. As a boy he would often go on hikes and collect interesting plants and animals to take back to examine with his dad.

Pierre was schooled at home. First, his mother taught him. Later he studied with his father and his brother Jacques, who was three years older. Pierre was a bit of a dreamer, so being taught at home was a blessing. It took him a while to process information. Once he did understand a concept, though, it would be crystal clear to him.

When Pierre was fourteen his parents enrolled him in the Faculty of Sciences at the Sorbonne. He began studying with Professor A. Bazille, who tutored him in mathematics and physics. Bazille saw the young man's potential. The two became very close. Pierre blossomed under the teacher's attention. He was able to earn a degree in math when he was just sixteen years old. Two years later, he had earned another degree in physics. In 1878, Pierre was offered a job as a laboratory assistant in the Sorbonne's physics lab. He would have preferred to continue with his studies, but he couldn't afford to keep going to school. He accepted the position.

Pierre used his access to the lab to work on a number of experiments. For three years he worked with crystals. He studied infrared rays. He was especially pleased that his brother also worked at the Sorbonne. They spent hours together working in the lab.

In 1880, the Curie brothers discovered something interesting about crystals. When certain crystals are compressed, they produce a small electrical charge. Called piezoelectricity, it was a significant finding. Piezoelectricity would be used in many ways, including in microphones and speakers.

But their days of professional collaboration would be short-lived. Jacques accepted a new position as a mineralogy professor at the University of Montpelier. In 1883, Pierre was appointed director of laboratory work of the Paris Municipal School of Industrial Physics and Chemistry. It was there that he began his pioneering work on magnetism. One of his discoveries was to establish the relationship between temperature and magnetic materials. As the temperature goes up, materials become less magnetic. The temperature at which a substance's magnetic properties disappear altogether is now known as the Curie point.

But Pierre also enjoyed life outside the laboratory. He liked going to concerts, to art exhibits, and for long walks along the Seine River, which runs through Paris. He also dabbled in poetry.

What shall I become?
Very rarely have I command of all myself; ordinarily a part of me sleeps.
My poor spirit, are you then so weak that you cannot control my body?
Oh, my thoughts, you count indeed for very little!
I should have the greatest confidence in the power of my imagination to pull me out of the rut, but I greatly fear that my imagination is dead.[1]

Despite being a thoughtful, sensitive man, Pierre doubted he would ever get married. When he was twenty-two, he wrote the following entry in his journal:

Women, much more than men, love life for life's sake. Women of genius are rare. And when, pushed by some mystic love, we wish to enter into a life opposed to nature, when we give all our thoughts to some work which removes us from those immediately about us, it is with women that we have to struggle, and the struggle is nearly always an unequal one. For in the name of life and of nature they seek to lead us back.[2]

Curie did have one girlfriend a few years after writing the entry. She later died tragically. By the time he reached his mid-thirties, Pierre had settled into a comfortable, if occasionally lonely, life of bachelorhood. His life was about to take an unexpected turn.

In 1894, Marie Sklodowska had already earned a degree in physics. She was working as a research assistant and had mentioned to an acquaintance that she was looking for lab space. The fellow physicist happened to be a friend of Pierre's. One night, he invited Marie over to his house. He also invited Pierre. Later, Marie would recall, "As I entered the room, Pierre Curie was standing in the recess of a French window opening on a balcony. He seemed to me very young, though he was at that time thirty-five years old. I was struck by the open expression of his face and by the slight suggestion of detachment in his whole attitude. His speech, rather slow and deliberate, his simplicity, and his smile, at once grave and youthful, inspired confidence."[3]

Both Marie and Pierre were normally shy, but they spent the entire evening talking. She told him about her difficulties finding appropriate workspace. Later, Pierre found her a small lab space at the Municipal School. He also started finding reasons to visit Marie's lab. Curie felt an exhilarating kinship with Marie, who was eight years younger than he. Eventually, he asked if he could visit her outside the lab. He would come to her small rented room. They would talk for hours about their mutual desire to live a life of scientific research. In his heart, Pierre knew he had finally found a soul mate. Marie understood, and shared, his passion for research and science.

What began as a professional association grew into a personal, romantic relationship. That summer, Marie took a vacation to Poland to visit her father. When she had first gone to Paris, she had intended to stay only temporarily. She had planned to return to Poland to be a teacher after finishing school. She was still torn about leaving her father alone. But throughout her vacation, Pierre wrote her long love letters. He convinced her to return to Paris and work toward her doctorate degree, or Ph.D.

"It would, nevertheless, be a beautiful thing in which I hardly dare believe, to pass through life together hypnotized in our dreams: your dream for your country; our dream for humanity; our dream for science," Pierre wrote. Always the scientist, he added, "I strongly advise you to return to Paris in October. I shall be very unhappy if you do not come this year, but it is not my friend's selfishness that makes me ask you to return. I ask it because I believe you will work better here and that you can accomplish here something more substantial and more useful."[4]

In July 1895, Pierre and Marie were married at Sceaux, where Pierre's parents lived. They used the money they were given as a wedding present to buy two bicycles. Their bike rides became their favorite way to relax and unwind together. It was about their only recreation. Most of their time was spent working or studying. But their marriage signaled the beginning of a personal and professional partnership that would literally change the world.

After their marriage, Marie and Pierre Curie were inseparable. They worked together and spent all their free time together. Their favorite pastime was riding their bikes, which they had bought as a wedding present to themselves. They spent so much time in the laboratory that it became their only exercise and the best way for them to relax.

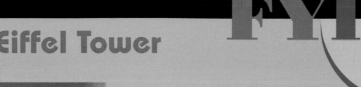

The Eiffel Tower

When Marie moved to Paris in 1891, the Eiffel Tower was just two years old. Over 700 designs had been proposed for the monument. It was to be built in 1889 as part of the Universal Exhibition (like a World's Fair). That year also happened to be the hundredth anniversary of the start of the French Revolution. It had been suggested to build a giant guillotine to honor the event, but that idea was voted down in favor of something less gruesome. The design by famed architect Gustave Eiffel was the final choice. Surprisingly, not everyone was impressed with the idea of the tower. A petition was circulated protesting its construction but failed to prevent Eiffel from going forward.

It took 300 steelworkers two years to build the tower. Rising to a height of one thousand feet, it was the world's tallest building at the time. In honor of the occasion, the Prince of Wales, who would later be crowned King Edward VII of England, participated in the opening ceremonies.

In the years following the exhibition, the tower continued to struggle to be accepted. In 1909, it was almost torn down. It was spared only because the telegraph antenna on top was deemed too valuable to lose. In later years the tower was used for radio and television antennas.

The tower is Eiffel's most famous work, but he worked on many projects throughout his life. He built bridges, train stations, canals, and the Statue of Liberty. Working alongside sculptors Auguste Bartholdi and Richard M. Hunt, Eiffel designed the statue's iron skeleton. He also determined how to properly distribute its weight by calculating how much pressure to put on each joint. And he supervised the raising of the statue once it reached New York.

Marie poses for a family portrait with her father, Vladislav Sklodowska, and sisters Bronia and Helena. Even though it was forbidden for girls to attend college in Poland, Vladislav believed it was important for his daughters to be educated and encouraged Maria and Bronia to move to Paris to continue their studies.

4

A Momentous Discovery

Pierre published a number of important papers, but other French scientists considered him an outsider. He had yet to complete his doctorate. Without that advanced degree, he was unable to get a job at any of the top French universities. Marie and Pierre's father finally convinced him to finish his thesis. In it he presented the correlation between temperature and magnetism that is now known as Curie's law.

In September 1897, Marie gave birth to their first child, Irène. Marie had finished her study of the magnetic properties of steel. She decided to work on her own doctoral thesis. She just had to decide on a subject. When she came across the work of Henri Becquerel, she knew her search was over.

Science is an ongoing process of discovery. Most advances in science are based on the work of others. For example, Roentgen discovered X-rays by observing the fluorescence they produced. Later, Becquerel decided to pursue his own investigation of these mysterious rays. Becquerel exposed a type of uranium ore called pitchblende. He placed it on photographic plates wrapped in black paper. When developed, the plates revealed an image of the uranium crystals. Becquerel concluded that the sun's energy was being absorbed by the uranium, which then emitted X-rays.

The next two days were cloudy. Becquerel believed the sun was necessary to continue his experiments. He put the plates and the uranium in

French physicist Henri Becquerel's work with X-rays helped lead Marie Curie to the discovery of radioactivity. Becquerel determined that the radiation in uranium was made up of charged particles. In 1903, he would be awarded the Nobel Prize in Physics along with Marie and Pierre Curie.

a drawer to wait for the next sunny day. Three days later he took them out of the drawer. To his surprise the images of the uranium were once again clear and strong, even though everything had been shut in a dark drawer. This meant that the uranium emitted radiation on its own. The sun had nothing to do with it. Becquerel would later show that the radiation emitted by uranium shared certain characteristics with X-rays. But unlike X-rays, these rays could be deflected by a magnetic field. Therefore, he concluded, uranium's radiation must consist of charged particles.

Marie was fascinated by Becquerel's findings. For her thesis she set out to discover if the property discovered in uranium could be found in other matter. Marie used some of the electrical instruments that Pierre had invented for his magnetism research. She was able to measure the particles emanating from her purified samples. She found that the same property was in the element thorium. As she continued her research, she made an unexpected discovery. She realized that the strength of the radiation did not depend on a chemical reaction. The strength depended only on the amount of uranium or thorium. More specifically, the ability to radiate, a process Marie termed radioactivity, occurred within the atom itself. This was completely revolutionary. At that time not all scientists even believed there were atoms, as we know there are today.

Uranium was discovered in 1789 by a German chemist named Martin Klaproth, who isolated it from the mineral called pitchblende. Uranium is a heavy metal that is radioactive. Its chemical symbol in the periodic table, as shown above, is "U." One of uranium's isotopes, U-235, was integral in the development of the atomic bomb.

Her next idea was to study the natural ores that contain uranium and thorium, such as pitchblende. When she measured the radiation from pitchblende, she found it was almost five times as active as uranium. The obvious conclusion was that there must be some undiscovered element in pitchblende that also emitted radiation. It was at this point that Pierre joined Marie in her research. Pierre Curie devoted himself chiefly to the physical study of the new radiations. Marie Curie worked painstakingly to isolate the substance.

Finally, in June 1898, Marie and Pierre had isolated a substance that emitted three hundred times more radiation than uranium. In their published paper on the discovery, they wrote: "We thus believe that the substance that we have extracted from pitchblende contains a metal never known before, akin to bismuth in its analytic properties. If the existence of this new metal is confirmed, we suggest that it should be called polonium after the name of the country of origin of one of us."[1] Five months later, the Curies announced they had found a second mysterious radioactive element in pitchblende, which they called radium.

What makes their discoveries even more amazing is that they were working in terrible living conditions. The only lab at their disposal was drafty and run down. It had a dirt floor. During the winter it was freezing cold. One colleague described it as looking more like a stable or potato cellar than a proper laboratory. But Marie and Pierre hardly seemed to notice. The soft glow from all the radioactive material in their lab had an almost hypnotic effect. She would later write in her memoir, "One of our pleasures was to enter our workshop at night; then, all around us, we would see the luminous silhouettes of the beakers and capsules that contained our products."[2] Marie even kept a vial of radium salts on the stand next to her bed at home. She liked to see its blue glow.

Pierre and Marie did not have much money. But, like Roentgen, they refused to file a patent application on their discoveries. They believed it was more important for other scientists to have the freedom to build upon their work. The betterment of humanity was more important to them than financial gain.

In 1903, Marie earned her doctorate. She had proved her original thesis and so much more. The importance of her work in radioactivity can only be truly appreciated in retrospect. It can be argued that her work was the start of the atomic age. It paved the way for modern physics, including the theory of quantum mechanics. Even if the full

X-rays were discovered by German physics professor Wilhelm Conrad Roentgen in 1895. Roentgen was awarded the Nobel Prize in Physics in 1901 for his work with X-rays. A devout humanitarian, Roentgen refused to patent his work believing it was more important for scientists to be able to use his discovery and its application for the betterment of mankind.

importance of the Curies' discoveries wasn't entirely understood, they were still considered a remarkable achievement. Shortly after the Curies announced their discoveries, the Royal Society of London honored them with the Davy medal. It is given annually for an outstandingly important recent discovery in any branch of chemistry made in Europe or North America. Marie and Pierre were then honored with the ultimate recognition, the 1903 Nobel Prize in physics, which they shared with Becquerel. Becquerel was awarded "in recognition of the extraordinary services he has rendered by his discovery of spontaneous radioactivity."[3] The Curies were awarded "in recognition of the extraordinary services they have rendered by their joint researches on the radiation phenomena discovered by Professor Henri Becquerel."[4]

Finally, it seemed their days of struggle were over. The Nobel Prize includes a large sum of money. Also, Pierre had been hired as the chair of physics at the University of Paris. The Curie family was finally able to live a more comfortable lifestyle. In December 1904, Marie gave birth to their second daughter, Eve.

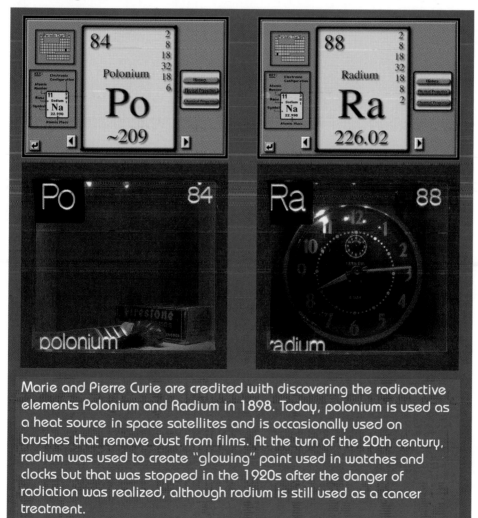

Marie and Pierre Curie are credited with discovering the radioactive elements Polonium and Radium in 1898. Today, polonium is used as a heat source in space satellites and is occasionally used on brushes that remove dust from films. At the turn of the 20th century, radium was used to create "glowing" paint used in watches and clocks but that was stopped in the 1920s after the danger of radiation was realized, although radium is still used as a cancer treatment.

33

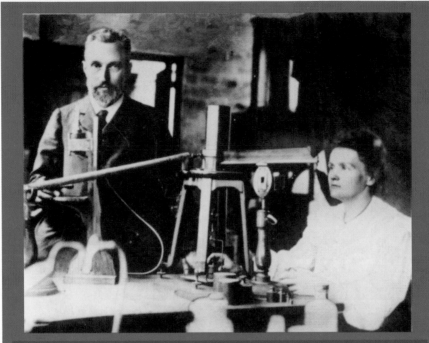

Although Marie and Pierre loved looking at the glow given off by the radioactive material in their lab, working with radium would cause them health problems. Pierre suffered burns from his skin coming into contact with radium, and their hands were in constant pain from the years of handling radioactive materials. Today, scientists use protective clothing, but during the Curie's day, nobody knew the long term dangers of radioactivity.

As the public learned about their discoveries, radium became considered a kind of miracle drug. Doctors began treating tumors with the radioactive element. The procedure was called Curietherapy. Facial creams containing thorium and radium were sold to promote healthy skin. What wasn't publicized were the harmful effects both Marie and Pierre had experienced. During their research, Pierre had put radium on his skin and experienced painful burns. The fingertips of both scientists were permanently scarred. They throbbed in constant pain from handling the radioactive samples. Marie was chronically tired. More tragically, in 1903 Marie had suffered a miscarriage in her fifth month of pregnancy. The miscarriage was probably due to radiation exposure. Some people would later blame the ill effects of radiation for another accident that would change Marie's life forever.

Just as words are made up of different letter combinations, everything in nature is made up of combinations of elements. Elements are substances that can't be broken down into simpler substances. Oxygen, uranium, and sodium are examples of elements. All elements have different properties. They can be liquid, solid, and gas. Over time, scientists noticed that some elements seem to share certain characteristics with other elements. But they didn't fully understand what those relationships were. Then Dmitri Ivanovich Mendeleyev developed a chart to categorize elements.

Mendeleyev was born in Siberia in 1834. He grew up to be a chemistry professor at the University of St. Petersburg. He was unhappy with the textbooks then available, so he wrote one of his own. While working on it, he made an interesting discovery. He found that groups of elements had similar properties that occurred in a pattern. He called that pattern a period.

Today we know there are over 110 elements. In Mendeleyev's day only 63 elements had been identified. He arranged the elements known at the time in order of increasing atomic weight, with repetitions after definite intervals. By setting up this chart, he was able to predict where as-yet-undiscovered elements would fit. Because of this work, Mendeleyev is considered to be the Father of the Periodic Table.

Dmitri Ivanovich Mendeleyev

Over time, scientists realized Mendeleyev's arrangement of elements in order of atomic weight didn't quite work. Atomic weight is roughly equal to the number of protons plus neutrons in the nucleus. In 1913 British physicist Henry Moseley suggested atomic weight wasn't the key to organizing the elements' properties. What really matters is each element's atomic number. Atomic number refers to the number of electrons its atom carries. Moseley was able to measure atomic number using X-rays. Ever since his discovery, elements have been arranged on the periodic table according to their atomic numbers.

During her life, Marie Curie was the most famous woman scientist in the world. She became the first female professor at the prestigious Sorbonne and people traveled from all over Europe to hear her lectures. But despite her achievements, Marie Curie faced resentment from many of her male colleagues.

5

A Scientific Legacy

Pierre Curie used to carry radium around in his pocket. He liked to show people how it glowed. He would sometimes boast that radium was a million times more powerful than uranium. Today, no scientist would intentionally expose himself to radioactive elements. But in the early twentieth century, the devastating effects of long-term radiation exposure weren't fully understood. By 1906, Pierre's health had noticeably deteriorated. He was weak. At times his legs shook. And the pain in his back was so severe that he could barely stand up straight. He told Marie he didn't think he would be coming to the lab much anymore. Marie herself was spending more time at home taking care of their two young children.

On April 19 Pierre was out by himself, walking in the Latin Quarter. It was raining. He stepped off a curb on a busy street. He didn't see an oncoming horse-drawn carriage. He was thrown to the ground and run over. He died instantly.

Marie suddenly found herself a widow and single mother of two. She was thirty-eight years old. She was devastated, but she was determined to continue with their life's work. Now she would dedicate her work to Pierre's memory.

The university appointed Marie to take Pierre's place as professor of physics at the Sorbonne. She was the first woman to be named professor at the school. When Curie gave her first lecture, the auditorium was packed. In addition to students, members of the press attended. When Marie walked in, she received a standing ovation. The audience honored her both for being the first female professor and for all her achievements.

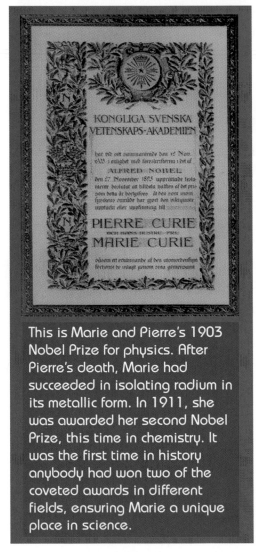

This is Marie and Pierre's 1903 Nobel Prize for physics. After Pierre's death, Marie had succeeded in isolating radium in its metallic form. In 1911, she was awarded her second Nobel Prize, this time in chemistry. It was the first time in history anybody had won two of the coveted awards in different fields, ensuring Marie a unique place in science.

Marie was happy to have a steady income, but she struggled to juggle her work with motherhood. Her family then suffered another tragedy. Pierre's father died. He had been living with her and had helped with the kids. Marie hired a young Polish woman as a live-in governess. That allowed Marie to continue her work. At first, it was a difficult transition. Marie missed Pierre. She missed him as her husband at home. She missed him as her research partner at work. One of her longtime lab assistants, André Debierne, became her new collaborator. He worked with Marie as she succeeded in isolating radium in metallic form. In 1910 her fundamental treatise on radioactivity was published. A year later she was awarded her second Nobel Prize. This time she won in chemistry, "in recognition of her services to the advancement of chemistry by the discovery of the elements radium and polonium, by the isolation of radium and the study of the nature and compounds

of this remarkable element."[1] It was the first time anyone had won two Nobel Prizes in different fields.

To facilitate her work, the Sorbonne agreed to build the Radium Institute, a state-of-the art laboratory for Marie. To help pay for the research conducted by the Institute and make it a world class center, Marie helped raise money by personally soliciting potential donors and giving magazine interviews to explain the important work being done there.

The second Nobel Prize made Marie even more famous. The Sorbonne agreed to build a state-of-the-art laboratory for her. Construction took five long years. In 1914, the laboratories of the Radium Institute were completed. The institute had two buildings. One building was the Curie Pavilion for physics and mathematics research. Marie would oversee the work in that building. The other building was the Pasteur Pavilion for biomedical research. It was named after Louis Pasteur.

During World War I Marie turned her energies toward helping soldiers. She advocated using X-rays on the wounded. The X-rays could locate bullets and shrapnel. This would make surgery easier. It also helped prevent countless amputations. Since the wounded often could not be moved, Marie invented X-ray vans. She trained 150 female attendants as radiologists. After the war, she devoted her energies to running the Curie Institute. She spent time raising money needed to fund its research. She made several

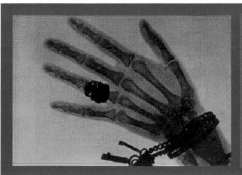

This is the first X-ray ever taken, made by Roentgen of his wife's hand. The picture accompanied the scientific paper Roentgen presented of his findings. Considered a medical miracle, X-rays quickly became an important diagnostic tool for doctors, allowing them to see inside the body of a living patient.

In 1995, the French government moved the remains of Marie and Pierre Curie to the country's national mausoleum, the Panthéon, located in Paris. Once again, Marie was a pioneer, being the first woman buried at the Pantheon on the basis of her own accomplishments. Pictured left is the plaque commemorating the couple.

trips to the United States to raise money. She secured underwriting from steel industrialist Andrew Carnegie, the richest man in the world.

In the late 1920s, Marie's health began to worsen noticeably. She suffered from tinnitus, a constant ringing and humming in her ears. She also experienced chronic pain similar to Pierre's. She developed cataracts. All these were symptoms of radiation poisoning.

Marie refused to let her ailments get the best of her. In 1932 she and her daughters visited the Grand Canyon. She even took a mule ride to the bottom. Back home in Paris, Marie still went to the lab when she was feeling strong enough. When she stayed home, she kept busy working on her book, *Radioactivity.* One afternoon in May 1934, Marie went home sick. She would never return to the lab. Although she had a myriad of ailments, none of the specialists could pinpoint a specific cause. Eventually she was diagnosed with leukemia. There was no cure. The disease was no doubt the result of years of radiation exposure.

Marie Curie died on July 4, 1934. She was buried in the same cemetery in Sceaux where Pierre had been laid to rest. Sixty years later the Curies' remains were moved to France's national mausoleum, the Panthéon, in Paris. Marie was the first woman to be granted the honor based on her own accomplishments. French President François Mitterand spoke at the 1995 interment ceremony. "By transferring these ashes of Pierre and Marie Curie into the sanctuary of our collective memory, France not only performs an act of recognition, it also affirms a faith in science, in research, and its respect for those who dedicate themselves to science, just as Pierre and Marie Curie dedicated their energies and their lives to science."[2]

But the Curie legacy didn't end there. A year after her mother's death, Irène would win the family's third Nobel Prize. She won in the chemistry category, for her work in synthesizing new radioactive elements. Marie and Irène are the only mother-daughter Nobel Prize winners in history.

The Curie family made Nobel history a third time in 1935 when eldest daughter Irène Joliot-Curie won the Nobel Prize in chemistry for her work in nuclear research which led to the discovery that radioactive elements can be artificially made using stable elements. Marie and Irene remain the only mother-daughter Nobel winners in history.

Despite the dangers it poses, radium has also been used to benefit mankind. After its discovery, radium was used to treat cancers by applying beams of radiation to the diseased tissue. By 1910 the treatment had gained widespread acceptance. During the early twentieth century, radium was one of the most valuable elements on earth. In 1906, a gram of radium was worth the equivalent of $10 million. Over the years, more economical, more powerful artificial radioisotopes such as cobalt-60 and cesium-137 have replaced it.

Because it glows, radium was used as an ingredient in a luminescent paint that was used on watches, clocks, and instrument dials. Factory workers who applied the paint would often wet the paintbrushes by putting them in their mouths. It wasn't until their teeth started falling out that workers began to suspect something in the paint was endangering their health. They also suffered from severe anemia. X-rays revealed they suffered from extensive bone decay.

In 1917, two doctors founded the Radium Luminous Materials Corporation in Orange, New Jersey. It was later renamed the U.S. Radium Corporation. The company refined radium and produced radium-based paints. The company stopped processing radium in 1926. They were sued by employees who claimed their various health problems had been caused by the radiation they had been exposed to in the workplace. Those suspicions were eventually verified in the 1930s. Eventually, it was proven just how significant a health hazard radiation was. Since then highly radioactive materials for commercial uses have been restricted.

The facility that housed the U.S. Radium Corporation was sold in the late 1940s. However, the radiation lingered on. In 1983, the site was still radioactive, and it was included on the Superfund National Priorities List. The list identifies areas that pose hazards to the environment and require special decontamination.

Chronology

1859	Pierre Curie is born in Paris, France, on May 15.
1867	Maria Sklodowska is born in Warsaw, Poland, on November 7.
1873	Pierre begins studying with Professor A. Bazille at the Sorbonne.
1875	Pierre earns a degree in math.
1877	Pierre earns a degree in physics.
1878	Pierre is hired as a laboratory assistant in the Sorbonne's physics lab.
1880	Pierre and his brother, Jacques, discover piezoelectricity.
1883	Maria graduates first in her high school class. Pierre is appointed director of laboratory work of the Paris Municipal School of Physics and Industrial Chemistry, where he begins his pioneering work on magnetism.
1886	Maria takes a job as a governess.
1891	Maria moves to Paris to enroll in the Sorbonne; she changes her name to Marie.
1894	Marie graduates from the Sorbonne with mathematics honors; she begins working as a research assistant for Gabriel Lippmann; she meets Pierre Curie.
1895	Marie and Pierre marry.
1897	Their daughter Irène is born on September 12.
1898	Marie and Pierre isolate polonium and radium.
1903	Marie earns her Ph.D. She and Pierre, along with Henri Becquerel, are awarded the Nobel Prize for physics; Marie is the first woman to win a Nobel Prize.
1904	Their second daughter, Eve, is born in December.
1906	Pierre dies after being hit by a horse cart. Marie becomes the first woman hired to teach at the Sorbonne.
1911	Marie is awarded the Nobel Prize in chemistry for isolating radium. This is the first time anyone has won two Nobel Prizes in different fields.
1914	Marie opens the Radium Institute, which includes the Curie Pavilion.
1934	Marie dies on July 4.

43

Timeline of Discovery

1854	Florence Nightingale tends to wounded soldiers during the Crimean War.
1869	Dmitri Mendeleyev publishes his Periodic Table of the Elements.
1876	Alexander Graham Bell invents the telephone.
1879	Thomas Edison invents the lightbulb.
1887	Heinrich Hertz discovers radio waves.
1895	William Roentgen discovers X-rays.
1896	Radioactivity is discovered by Antoine-Henri Becquerel.
1897	Bayer's Felix Hoffmann develops pure acetylsalicylic acid, better known as aspirin.
1904	The Curies isolate a single gram of radium from eight tons of uranium residue; working with radium, Bertram Borden Boltwood discovers that one element can decay into another.
1905	Nettie Stevens announces discovery that the X- and Y-chromosomes are responsible for determining gender.
1910	Marie Curie publishes her treatise on radioactivity.
1913	Henry Moseley uses X-ray diffraction to establish the significance of atomic number.
1916	Einstein postulates his general theory of relativity.
1917	The Russian Revolution begins.
1919	Ernest Rutherford discovers the proton.
1928	Bubble gum invented by Walter E. Diemer.
1934	Irène Joliot-Curie and Frédéric Joliot synthesize new radioactive elements.
1938	Hitler invades Austria; Otto Hahn and Fritz Strassmann discover nuclear fission.
1943	The world's first operational nuclear reactor is activated at Oak Ridge, Tennessee.
1945	Hiroshima and Nagasaki, Japan, are destroyed by the first atomic bomb used in warfare.
1951	Rosalind Franklin discovers the double-helix shape of the DNA molecule, a finding later used by James Watson and Francis Crick in building the DNA model.
1952	The world's first thermonuclear device—the H-bomb—is detonated.
2004	Aaron Ciechanover, Avram Hershko, and Irwin Rose win the 2004 Nobel Prize for chemistry.

Chapter Notes

Chapter One   A Deadly Accident
1. Viktor Haynes and Marko Bojcun, *The Chernobyl Disaster: The True Story of a Catastrophe—An Unanswerable Indictment of Nuclear Power* (London: The Hogarth Press, 1988), p. 9.

Chapter Two   Early Loss
1. Naomi Pasachoff, *Marie Curie and the Science of Radioactivity* (Oxford: Oxford University Press, 1996). Online at http://www.aip.org/history/curie/contents.htm
2. Marie Curie, *Pierre Curie and Autobiographical Notes* (New York: The Macmillan Company, 1923), p. 159.
3. Pasachoff.
4. Ibid.
5. Curie, p. 166.
6. Ibid., p. 171.

Chapter Three   Magnetic Attraction
1. Marie Curie, *Pierre Curie and Autobiographical Notes* (New York: The Macmillan Company, 1923), p. 46.
2. Ibid., p. 77.
3. Ibid., p. 68.
4. Ibid., p. 76.

Chapter Four   A Momentous Discovery
1. Marie Curie Fellowship Association Annals, n.d., http://www.mariecurie.org/annals/index.html?frame3=/annals/volume2/call.html
2. Marie Curie, *Pierre Curie and Autobiographical Notes* (New York: The Macmillan Company, 1923), p. 104.
3. "The Nobel Prize in Physics 1903," http://www.nobel.se/physics/laureates/1903/press.html
4. Ibid.

Chapter Five   A Scientific Legacy
1. "The Nobel Prize in Physics 1911," http://www.nobel.se/physics/laureates/1911/press.html
2. *Marie Curie and the Science of Radioactivity*, "The Radium Institute, 1919–1934," http://www.aip.org/history/curie/radinst3.htm

Glossary

alpha particle   (AL-fa PAR-ti-cul)—a particle emitted from the nucleus of an atom; it contains two protons and two neutrons.

anemia   (ah-NEE-mee-ah)—a disease that affects the blood's ability to deliver oxygen around the body.

beta particle   (BAY-tah)—a high-speed particle, identical to an electron, emitted from an atomic nucleus.

chronic exposure   (KRAH-nik ek-SPOE-jur)—repeated exposure to radioactivity over a long period of time.

contamination   (con-tah-mih-NAY-shun)—the presence of harmful radioactive substances where they are not supposed to be.

czar   (ZAR)—a title referring to any of the Russian emperors, who ruled until the revolution of 1917.

decontamination   (DEE-con-tah-mih-NAY-shun)—the removal or reduction of contamination on people or in the environment.

dose   (dohse)—a measure of radiation absorbed by a person or object.

element   (EL-uh-ment)—the simplest part into which something can be divided.

exposure   (ek-SPOE-zur)—contact with radiation.

gamma ray   (GA-muh ray)—a type of radiation emitted from an atom's nucleus.

isotope   (EYE-suh-tope)—one of two or more types of a chemical element that have the same atomic number but a different atomic mass.

nucleus   (NEW-klee-us)—the center of an atom that contains most of its mass. In all elements except hydrogen, the nucleus is made up of protons and neutrons.

pitchblende   (PITCH-blend)—one of the primary mineral ores of uranium. Three radioactive elements were first discovered in pitchblende: uranium, polonium, and radium.

polonium   (po-LO-nee-um)—a radioactive, silvery-gray or black metallic element first discovered in 1898 by Pierre and Marie Curie.

radiation   (ray-dee-AY-shun)—a form of energy that can be categorized according to wavelength; the spectrum includes X-rays, radio waves, and infrared, ultraviolet, and visible light.

radiation sickness   (ray-dee-AY-shun SICK-ness)—an illness caused by excessive doses of radiation.

radioactivity   (RAY-dee-oh ack-TI-vi-tee)—the spontaneous emission of radiation, normally alpha or beta particles often accompanied by gamma rays, from the nucleus of an unstable isotope.

radium   (ray-dee-um)—a silvery, soft radioactive element found naturally in uranium and thorium ores.

x-ray   (EX-ray)—a type of electromagnetic radiation, between ultraviolet light and gamma rays.

For Further Reading

For Young Adults

Fullick, Ann. *Marie Curie*. Groundbreakers—Scientists & Inventors. Chicago: Heinemann Library, 2003.

McGrayne, Sharon Bertsch. *Nobel Prize Women in Science: Their Lives, Struggles, and Momentous Discoveries*. New York: Carol Press, 1993.

Pasachoff, Naomi. *Marie Curie and the Science of Radioactivity*. New York and Oxford: Oxford University Press, 1996.

Pflaum, Rosalynd. *Grand Obsession: Madame Curie and Her World*. New York: Doubleday, 1989.

Poynter, Margaret. *Marie Curie: Discoverer of Radium*. Berkeley Heights, NJ: Enslow Publishers, Inc., 2001.

Rayner-Canham, Marlene and Geoffrey. *A Devotion to Their Science: Pioneer Women of Radioactivity*. Montreal: McGill-Queen's University Press, 1997.

Steinke, Anne E. *Marie Curie and the Discovery of Radium*. Hauppauge, NY: Barron's Children's Books, 1987.

Works Cited

Crawford, Elisabeth. *The Beginnings of the Nobel Institution, The Science Prizes 1901–1915*. Cambridge: Cambridge University Press, & Paris: Edition de la Maison des Sciences, 1984.

Curie, Eve. *Madame Curie*. Paris: Gallimard, 1938; in English, New York: Doubleday.

Curie, Marie. *Pierre Curie* and *Autobiographical Notes*. New York: The Macmillan Company, 1923. (Subsequently Marie Curie refused to authorize publication of her *Autobiographical Notes* in any other country.)

Giroud, Françoise, and Lydia Davis (translator). *Marie Curie, a Life*. New York: Holmes & Meier, 1986.

Haynes, Viktor, and Marko Bojcun. *The Chernobyl Disaster: The True Story of a Catastrophe—An Unanswerable Indictment of Nuclear Power*. London: The Hogarth Press, 1988.

McGrayne, Sharon Bertsch. *Nobel Prize Women in Science: Their Lives, Struggles and Momentous Discoveries*. New York: Carol Press, 1993.

Nobel Lectures, including Presentation Speeches and Laureates' Biographies, Physics 1901–21. Published for the Nobel Foundation in 1967 by Elsevier Publishing Company, Amsterdam-London-New York.

Nobel Lectures, including Presentation Speeches and Laureates' Biographies, Chemistry 1901–21. Published for the Nobel Foundation in 1967 by Elsevier Publishing Company, Amsterdam-London-New York.

Pflaum, Rosalynd. *Grand Obsession: Madame Curie and Her World*. New York: Doubleday, 1989.

Quinn, Susan. *Marie Curie: A Life*. Simon & Schuster, New York, 1995.

Ramstedt, Eva. *Marie Sklodowska Curie*. Kosmos. Papers on Physics (in Swedish), published by Svenska Fysikersamfundet, no. 12, 1934.

Reid, Robert. *Marie Curie*. London: William Collins Sons & Co., Ltd., 1974.

On the Internet

Fröman, Nanny. "Marie and Pierre Curie and the Discovery of Polonium and Radium." Translated by Nancy Marshall-Lundén—
http://www.nobel.se/physics/articles/curie/index.html

Greenwald, John. "Deadly Meltdown." *Time*, May 12, 1986—http://www.time.com/time/daily/chernobyl/860512.cover.html

LaMotte, Larry. "CNN Presents Chernobyl: Legacy of a Meltdown." *CNN*, April 4, 1996—http://www.cnn.com/WORLD/9604/04/cnnp_chernobyl/index.html

Marie Curie and the Science of Radioactivity—http://www.aip.org/history/curie/polgirl2.htm

"Marie Curie: The Triumphs & Tragedies of a Scientific Career"—http://www.hypatiamaze.org/marie/curie_bio.html

U.S. Environmental Protection Agency—http://www.epa.gov/superfund/sites/

The World Almanac for Kids, "Marie Curie"—http://www.worldalmanacforkids.com/explore/inventions/curie_marie.html

Index